Real Estate License Exams for Beginners 2023

The Must-Have Guide to Ace Your Real Estate License Exams |
Proven Test-Taking Strategies to Get Your Foot in The Door of a
Successful Career

David M. Richeson

Table of contents

Introduction *4*

Chapter 1 What You Need To Know About Real Estate Agent Exams *8*

    A. Explanation of what real estate agent exams are 8

    B. Importance of passing the exams for becoming a licensed real estate agent 11

    II. Exam Requirements 13

    III. Exam Content 16

Chapter 2 Differences Between National And State Exams *20*

Chapter 3 Terminology You Need To Know *24*

    key terms and definitions used in the real estate industry 24

    Property Rights...30

    Zoning and Land Use Laws 31

    Contract Law 32

    Zoning and Land Use Regulations: 34

    Taxation 36

    Environmental Regulations 39

Chapter 5 Financial Aspects *42*

    Investment Cost...42

    Financing 45

Cash Flow 47

Appreciation 50

The Importance of Capital Appreciation 52

Market Conditions 52

Chapter 6 Legal aspects and contract types *55*

Purchase Agreement: 58

Listing Agreement: 59

Lease Agreement 62

Rental Agreement: 65

Option Agreement: 68

Chapter 7 Introduction about laws of most popular State *72*

Georgia 72

New Jersey 73

Connecticut 73

New York 73

California 73

Florida 74

Virginia 74

Washington 74

Texas 74

Illinois 75

South Carolina 75

North Carolina 75

Michigan 76

Tennessee 76

Indiana 76

Massachusetts 76

Chapter 8 Practice test...77

Conclusion: 88

Bonus 90

Introduction

The process of acquiring, selling, and owning land, buildings, and other structures, such as residential houses, places of business, and manufacturing facilities, are all examples of what is referred to as "real estate," and the phrase is used to characterise these activities. The purchasing, selling, renting, and leasing of these assets are all distinct sorts of real estate transactions that fall within the broader category of real estate business. The real estate industry is made up of many kinds of specialists who work together to make the buying, selling, and upkeep of properties feasible. Real estate agents, brokers, appraisers, and property managers are all examples of these types of professionals.

The ownership of a piece of land is essential to the real estate industry and is regarded as one of the sector's most significant traits. People who own their own property have the legal power to use, occupy, or otherwise dispose of a particular piece of land or structure in any way they see fit. This authority extends to all activities related to the property. The law offers protection for ownership rights, and the ownership of a piece of property can change hands either when the item is sold or when it is inherited according to the terms of a will. Both possible outcomes are in accordance with the law.

The real estate sector contains several essential components, one of which is financing. The process of acquiring a mortgage can be challenging and requires the participation of several stakeholders, such as the lender, the borrower, and the real estate agent. Before being able to acquire a house or any other kind of property, most people are forced to first secure a mortgage. When purchasing real estate, it is important to remember that there will be other costs, such as property taxes, insurance premiums, and maintenance fees, that need to be accounted for.

In addition, the business of real estate is overseen by a multitude of rules and regulations, some of which include zoning laws, laws addressing property taxes, and environmental limitations. These are only some of the regulations that affect the real estate industry. It is the job of real estate professionals to be knowledgeable about these laws and regulations to ensure that the transactions they perform are in conformity with any legal requirements that may be applicable.

When looking to buy or sell a piece of real estate, it is common practise to seek the aid of a real estate agent or broker to complete the transaction successfully. Real estate brokers aid their clients in the areas of buying, selling, and renting residential and commercial properties. They assist in the search for properties that fall within the client's price range and satisfy the client's criteria. Additionally, they assist in the negotiation of the transaction's terms, such as the price and the closing date. Brokers are licenced real estate professionals who have completed additional coursework and worked in the industry for a certain amount of time. In addition, they have the right to manage real estate transactions on their own.

In addition to the buying and selling of real estate, the administration of properties of all different kinds is a part of the real estate industry. These properties can range from residential to commercial to industrial in nature. The property managers oversee the day-to-day operations of these properties. They are responsible for the collecting of rent, the upkeep of the property, and the monitoring of tenants to ensure that they are following to the terms and conditions of their lease agreements.

A substantial amount of importance is also placed on the process of property evaluation in the real estate industry. The determination of the value of real estate for the purposes of real estate transactions, mortgage finance, and the assessment of property taxes is the domain of appraisers, who are highly educated and experienced professionals. When trying to determine the value of a piece of real estate, they will use a range of methods, such as completing an inspection of the property's condition and taking into consideration the features of the market in the region. Both are important factors.

The commercial and residential real estate market has a major impact on the economy. Real estate transactions are a significant driver of economic activity, and the real estate industry is responsible for the provision of employment opportunities for a diverse range of specialised workers, including real estate brokers, appraisers, property managers, and real estate agents. The possible increase in value of a homeowner's house and other real estate assets over the course of their lifetime can be a significant contributor to their overall wealth. An additional potential source of revenue for investors might come from owning real estate assets.

Chapter 1

What You Need To Know About Real Estate Agent Exams

A. Explanation of what real estate agent exams are

Exams for real estate agents are standardised examinations that are needed by most states in the United States to receive a licence to work as a real estate agent. Aspiring real estate agents are evaluated on their knowledge and abilities in a variety of domains connected to the real estate sector by means of these examinations. These domains include fundamental ideas and concepts, financial considerations, legal considerations, and terminology.

Exams to determine whether a person is qualified to work as a real estate agent are typically given by state-specific licencing authorities, such as state real estate boards or commissions. These exams are designed to determine whether an individual is qualified to work as a real estate agent. The examinations include a wide variety of disciplines, beginning with fundamental real estate ideas and progressing to more complex areas like as property valuation, financing, and contract law.

Protecting customers is one of the most important focuses of the examinations that real estate agents are required to take. The state licencing authorities want to ensure that licenced real estate agents have a minimum level of knowledge and competency in their field. This helps to prevent fraud, misrepresentation, and other unethical practises in real estate transactions. The state licencing authorities require individuals to pass the exams to ensure that this minimum level of knowledge and competency is met.

Individuals often need to satisfy specific criteria before being permitted to take the real estate agent tests. These requirements might include completing a pre-licensing course and acquiring a specified number of hours of real estate education before being authorised to take the exams. The pre-licensing course is a comprehensive educational programme that is designed to give prospective real estate agents with the core information they require to pass the examinations and eventually become licenced.

There is some variation in the structure of the real estate agent examinations from state to state; nevertheless, most exams are multiple-choice, computer-based tests that are frequently timed and given at testing centres. The length of the examinations varies depending on the state, but on average, candidates may expect to spend between two and four hours on each test.

Individuals have access to a range of study tools, including as textbooks, study guides, and online courses, which they may utilise to get ready for the real estate agent tests. They also have the option of taking practise examinations and mock tests, which will assist them in becoming accustomed to the structure and material covered on the real estate agent exams.

It is essential to arrive at the testing facility well-prepared and with sufficient time to spare while taking the examinations required to become a real estate agent. Aspiring real estate agents should also be familiar with the testing environment and the procedures for taking the exams, such as bringing a valid form of identification and avoiding bringing prohibited items into the testing room. Real estate agents are required to have a real estate licence to sell property.

The results of the real estate agent tests will be sent to candidates when they have completed the examinations. Individuals who wish to receive a licence to work as real estate agents in most states are required to demonstrate that they have achieved satisfactory results on both the national and state levels of the examinations. After a predetermined amount of time has passed, those who have attempted but failed the examinations may be given the opportunity to repeat the examinations.

After a person has received their real estate licence, they are required to participate in ongoing education to keep their licence active. Depending on the state, this may involve completing a specific number of hours of continuing education every year or once every few years.

Exams for real estate agents are the standardised examinations that must be passed by persons for them to be licenced as real estate agents. The tests are meant to safeguard customers by ensuring that licenced real estate agents have a minimal level of proficiency in their sector. They test the knowledge and abilities of prospective real estate agents in a variety of domains connected to the real estate industry. Persons can utilise study materials, practise examinations, and mock tests to prepare for the exams. In addition, individuals should arrive to the testing location well-prepared and with sufficient time to spare.

B. Importance of passing the exams for becoming a licensed real estate agent

To pursue a career in the real estate market and become a licenced real estate agent, it is very necessary to do well on the examinations required of prospective agents. The importance of achieving a passing score on the examinations may be broken down into numerous significant categories, including the following:

Legal Demand:

In most states, obtaining a licence to work as a real estate agent requires the candidate to demonstrate that they have obtained a passing score on the real estate agent tests. Persons who wish to work as real estate agents are required to complete the tests to receive a licence, and the exams are meant to examine the knowledge and abilities of individuals who are wanting to become real estate agents.

Demonstrating Competency:

The fundamental goal of the examinations that are required of real estate agents is to ensure the safety of the public. The state licencing authorities want to ensure that licenced real estate agents have a minimum level of knowledge and competency in their field. This helps to prevent fraud, misrepresentation, and other unethical practises in real estate transactions. The state licencing authorities require individuals to pass the exams to ensure that this minimum level of knowledge and competency is met.

Passing the examinations required to become a real estate agent is one method for individuals to demonstrate that they have the necessary skills and knowledge to work in the industry. Individuals can demonstrate to customers, colleagues, and future employers that they have the essential knowledge and abilities to provide professional real estate services by getting a licence, which allows them to do so.

Recognition as a Professional Standard Receiving a real estate licence after successfully completing the required coursework and examinations is a noteworthy accomplishment that is acknowledged as meeting a professional standard within the real estate business. Individuals can establish themselves as professional real estate agents and achieve recognition and respect in their business by acquiring a licence, which allows them to work in the sector legally.

Career Progression:

If you want to have a prosperous career in the real estate sector, the first thing you need to do is earn your real estate agent licence and then pass the real estate agent tests. After obtaining their licence, individuals can begin working as real estate agents and follow a variety of career paths, including selling residential or commercial properties, working in property management, or pursuing a career in real estate finance or appraisal.

Earning Potential:

Those who are licenced as real estate agents after successfully completing the necessary tests have the potential to make more money than their counterparts who are not licenced. Each real estate transaction in which a real estate agent is involved often results in the agent receiving a commission, and the more deals the agent can successfully close, the higher the agent's potential revenue.

The pursuit of a profession in real estate and the completion of the associated tests can be a trying but ultimately rewarding experience for one's personal growth.

The examinations contribute to the protection of consumers, the demonstration of competency, the provision of professional recognition, the progression of careers, and the opportunity for greater earnings. Individuals can get a significant amount of personally beneficial experience via the process of earning a licence by successfully completing the necessary examinations.

II. Exam Requirements

Individuals must first get a passing score on the state-mandated real estate agent tests to become licenced real estate agents in most states. There are some prerequisites that are standard throughout all states that persons must fulfil to be qualified to take the tests. However, the requirements for taking the exams differ slightly from state to state.

The following is a list of some of the most important prerequisites for the examination that persons need to be aware of:

Age Requirements:

Most states mandate that prospective real estate agents must be at least 18 years old before sitting for their licencing examinations. It's possible that various states have varying minimum wages for drivers, therefore individuals should check with the licencing office in their state to find out the precise criteria.

Education Requirements:

Education Prerequisites Before being allowed to take the examinations, persons are required by most states to have completed a specified amount of classroom instruction in real estate. The number of education hours required can range anywhere from 20 to 90 hours, depending on the state, with some jurisdictions needing as little as 20 hours and others requiring as many as 90.

Background Check:

Before being allowed to take the tests, people in most states are required to first pass a background check. A study of an individual's credit history and a check of their criminal history are both possible components of the background check. It is possible that individuals who have a history of unethical activity or specific criminal convictions will not be permitted to take the examinations.

Application and Fees:

For individuals to be allowed to take the examinations to become a real estate agent, they are required to first apply to the state licencing authority. The procedure of applying may require the submission of a fee in addition to the provision of personal and educational information. The costs associated with taking the tests can vary widely from one state to the next, with some jurisdictions costing as low as one hundred dollars while others charge several hundred.

Materials for Study In order to adequately prepare for the real estate agent tests, individuals are required to study not only the real estate principles of their state and the nation, but also the real estate rules and regulations that are particular to their own state. The term "study materials" can refer to a variety of resources, such as textbooks, study aids, and even online courses.

Exam Structure:

Scores Needed to Pass Although the scores needed to pass the real estate agent tests might differ from state to state, most states need candidates to get a score of at least 70 or 75 percent on the exams to pass. It's possible that residents of some states may need to pass not just their state test but also a national one, whereas residents of other states may simply need to pass their state exam.

Retake Policy:

Individuals who do not pass the real estate agent exams on their first attempt may be eligible to retake the exams; however, there may be restrictions on how soon they can retake the exams as well as how many times they can retake the exams. This applies to both the state and national levels of the exams.

Individuals are required to fulfil several essential prerequisites to be eligible to take the real estate agent tests, which are necessary to obtain a real estate agent licence. The prerequisites consist of the candidate's age, level of education, the results of a background check, the completion of an application and payment of any associated costs, the provision of study materials, the structure of the examination, the minimum score necessary to pass, and the In order to successfully take and pass the real estate agent tests, individuals should carefully research the standards that are required by their state and should be prepared to satisfy the criteria that are necessary.

III. Exam Content

Exams for real estate agents contain a wide variety of subjects connected to the fundamentals, procedures, and regulations of the real estate industry. The following is a list of some of the most important subjects that are likely to be covered in real estate agent exams:

Real Estate Principles:

The tests taken to become a real estate agent may contain questions on the fundamental principles of real estate, such as who owns the property, who has the rights to the property, and how much the property is worth. It is possible that individuals will be questioned about zoning rules, property taxes, and property rights to ascertain whether they comprehend these ideas.

Questions on mortgages:

other forms of loans, and interest rates may be included in the real estate agent tests that include the topic of finance. It is possible that people will be required to demonstrate their understanding of financial principles by providing responses to questions about matters such as the computation of mortgages, the amortisation of loans, and interest rates.

Questions on real estate law:

such as those pertaining to contracts, deeds, and property rights, could appear on the examinations required by real estate agents. It is possible that people will be required to show their understanding of legal ideas by providing responses to questions pertaining to subjects like property law, contract law, and fair housing legislation.

Questions regarding ethical standards in the real estate industry:

such as those pertaining to honesty, integrity, and the fair treatment of customers, might be included on the real estate agent tests. It is possible that people will be asked to demonstrate their familiarity with ethical concepts by providing responses to questions about subjects such as dual agency, conflicts of interest, and fair housing rules.

Mathematical Aspects of Real Estate:

The examinations taken by real estate agents may contain questions on mathematical aspects of real estate, such as property measurements, property taxes, and real estate computations. It is possible that individuals will be required to demonstrate their mastery of mathematical principles by responding to questions pertaining to themes such as the computation of property taxes, the computation of commissions, and the measuring of properties.

Real Estate Marketing:

There is a possibility that questions on real estate marketing will be included in the examinations required of real estate agents. These questions may focus on advertising, marketing strategies, or property presentations. It is possible for people to be asked to show their grasp of marketing ideas by answering questions on issues such as advertising regulations, property listings, and property presentations.

The real estate agent tests:

may include questions on the day-to-day operations of a real estate office, such as questions on office processes, customer interactions, and property management. These topics may also be included under the real estate operations category. It is possible that individuals will be asked to demonstrate their comprehension of real estate operations by responding to questions on a variety of subjects, including client interactions, office processes, and property management.

Questions on State-Specific Laws and Regulations:

The real estate agent tests could also include questions on state-specific laws and regulations, such as property disclosure laws, licencing requirements, and state-specific real estate practises. Examples of these topics include to ensure that they are adequately prepared for the examinations, individuals need become well-versed in the statutes and rules that are applicable to their state.

Exams for real estate agents contain a wide variety of subjects connected to the fundamentals, procedures, and regulations of the real estate industry. Questions in real estate fundamentals, finance, law, ethics, real estate arithmetic, real estate marketing, real estate operations, and state-specific rules and regulations could be on the tests. For individuals to be adequately prepared for the real estate agent tests, these subject areas should be studied in great depth.

Chapter 2

Differences Between National And State Exams

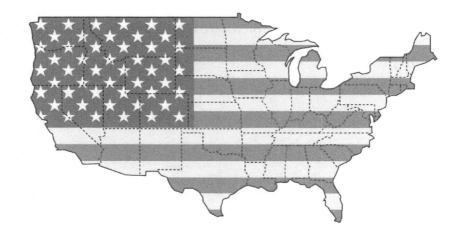

Both the national real estate agent examinations and the state-specific real estate agent exams have the same goal, which is to evaluate the candidates' level of expertise in terms of both their knowledge and their practical application of that information. However, there are several significant discrepancies between the two types of examinations about the content, format, and prerequisites.

The national real estate agent tests encompass a wide variety of subject matter that is associated with the fundamentals, procedures, and regulations of the real estate industry. The material included on the national tests could be of a broader character, and it might not include state-specific statutes and ordinances. On the other hand, state-specific exams are intended to test an individual's knowledge of state-specific laws and regulations in addition to the more general principles and practises of real estate. These exams are designed to test the individual's ability to apply real estate principles and practises.

Multiple-choice questions are by far the most frequent type of test style, so it's possible that all 50 states will use a structure that's quite like the one used for the national real estate agent examinations. On the other hand, the structure of state-specific tests may differ from one state to the next. While some states may use multiple-choice questions, others may use essay questions, and still others may use a combination of the two.

Individuals are needed to finish a pre-licensing course in addition to meeting any other qualifying criteria prior to take the national real estate agent tests. This is the case regardless of the state in which they reside. However, state-specific examinations may have varying prerequisites, such as a minimum age requirement, the need to submit fingerprints, pass a background check, and fulfil other qualifying conditions.

The national real estate agent tests and the state-specific real estate agent examinations serve a role that is comparable to one another, but they are distinct from one another in terms of their substance, structure, and prerequisites. State-specific tests are meant to evaluate an individual's knowledge of state-specific rules and regulations, whereas the national exams may be more generic in character and may not cover state-specific laws and regulations. There may be variations in the structure of the tests, with some states opting to use multiple-choice questions, some opting to use essay questions, and still others utilising a combination of both types of questions. In addition, the prerequisites for taking the tests might range from state to state. The qualifying requirements for the national exams can be very different from those of the state-specific exams.

Importance of studying state-specific material in addition to the material covered in the book

To become a licenced real estate agent, an individual is required to pass a thorough exam that examines their familiarity with the many concepts, practises, and laws pertaining to the real estate industry. It is vital to study the content that is included in the book on real estate agent tests; however, it is equally as important to learn the material that is relevant to your state.

Laws and Regulations That Are Unique to Each State Because real estate is a regulated industry at the state level, each state possesses its own unique body of laws and regulations that govern the industry. Because of the potential for these rules and regulations to be rather different from one state to the next, it is essential to have a solid understanding of them to operate real estate legally and ethically. If you study information that is particular to your state in addition to the content that is included in the book on real estate agent tests, you will be completely prepared for the state-specific examinations and will be able to pass them with flying colours.

Understanding the Local Market, the real estate market in the area is affected by several different elements, some of which include the local laws, rules, and traditions. You will be more able to counsel your customers and make educated decisions on their behalf if you study literature that is relevant to the state in where you work as a real estate agent. This will give you a deeper grasp of the local real estate market.

Gaining a deeper awareness of the local market as well as the state-specific rules and regulations can provide you a competitive edge in the real estate business, where the level of competition can be rather intense. You will be able to provide a greater level of service to your customers if you study content that is particular to the state, which may lead to a rise in both your business and your degree of success.

Completing the Necessary Steps to Obtain a License In order to obtain a licence in many states, individuals must first demonstrate that they have successfully completed both the national and state real estate agent tests. You will be able to successfully pass these examinations and fulfil the requirements for obtaining a licence to practise in the state in which you choose to do so if you study information that is particular to that state.

It is necessary, to become a licenced real estate agent, to study content that is particular to the state in addition to the material that is included in the book on real estate agent tests. It is crucial to understand these variations to practise real estate in a legal and ethical manner, provide a higher quality of service to your clients, and be successful in the field. The local real estate market, rules, and regulations might vary greatly from state to state. Additionally, in addition to the national real estate agent examinations, many states need persons to pass state-specific exams to get licenced as a real estate agent. If you study material that is unique to your state, you will be better prepared to satisfy these licencing criteria.

Chapter 3

Terminology You Need To Know

key terms and definitions used in the real estate industry

The myriad specialised terminology and ideas that are used in the real estate industry may sometimes be bewildering to those who are just starting out in the field of real estate as a profession. To be a successful real estate agent or professional, it is essential to have a comprehensive understanding of the industry's most important vocabulary and the connotations that are associated with it. These expressions and terminology are utilised consistently all over the sector. The following is a list of some of the most important terms and meanings that you need to be familiar with, and they are listed in alphabetical order:

An appraisal

An appraisal is simply an estimate as to how much money a piece of property is worth, but it is done for legal and financial purposes. During the assessment process, which is often carried out by certified appraisers, several factors, including the property's location, condition, and attributes, as well as market trends and transactions that are comparable to those at hand, are taken into consideration.

An agent

An agent is a licenced professional who is registered to do business in the real estate industry and is authorised to advise clients and negotiate real estate deals. In addition to this, brokers are accountable for maintaining open communication with their customers on the state of the market. Brokers have the option of going into business for themselves or finding employment with an existing brokerage firm.

Commission

Commission is the name given to the fee that is paid to a real estate agent in exchange for the services they provide throughout the process of acquiring or selling a piece of real estate. The commission is almost always calculated as a percentage of the final sales price of the property. This is the case in most situations.

The closing

The closing is the last step of a real estate transaction, and it is during this phase that all the necessary paperwork is signed by both the buyer and the seller, and control of the property is transferred from one party to the other. The buyer is responsible for paying any fees that are related with the closing, as well as any outstanding balances on the purchase price, when it comes time for the closing.

The expenses

The expenses that must be paid to complete the transaction are referred to as the closing costs. These expenditures might include the premiums for title insurance, the fees associated with an escrow account, and a wide range of other incidental goods.

An agreement

An agreement between a broker and their agents about the distribution of the money earned from the sale of real estate is known as a commission split. A commission split is the term used to describe this arrangement.

When purchasing real estate, the practise of putting monetary considerations into the care of a third party who is not involved in the transaction is referred to as "escrow." The party that is relevant to the transaction is granted access to the funds only after it has been verified that all the terms of the transaction have been met.

Listing Agreement:

A listing agreement is a contract between a property owner and a real estate agent in which the agent agrees to list the property for sale and the owner agrees to pay the agent a commission if the property sells. In this type of agreement, the agent agrees to list the property for sale and the owner agrees to pay the agent a commission. In this kind of contract, the owner of the property and the real estate agent both agree that the owner will pay the agent a commission for listing the property on the market.

Multiple Listing Service (MLS):

The Multiple Listing Service is a database that is kept up to date by real estate brokerages. This database contains listings of properties that are currently on the market and are available to be purchased. The Multiple Listing Service, abbreviated as "MLS," gives real estate agents access to a complete database of listings and makes it easier for them to share information with one another on different types of properties.

open house"

The term "open house" refers to a specific kind of event in which a house or other sort of property is displayed for the purpose of being viewed by potential buyers. Open houses are events that are frequently organised and hosted by real estate agents, and they provide prospective buyers the opportunity to visit the property in question and ask questions about it. Open houses are also known as "community events."

Disclosure of the Current Condition of the Property

The disclosure of the current state of a property is a document that may be required by law in certain areas. The owner of the property is obligated to disclose in this document any known issues or defects that are related with the property.

A real estate brokerage

A real estate brokerage is a firm that provides clients with several real estate services, including the listing and sale of residential and commercial properties. These services can be provided for both residential and commercial real estate. Real estate agents and brokers are frequently hired by brokerages, and the brokerages may also provide training and help for the agents that they employ. Real estate agents and brokers are typically employed by brokerages.

Licensed real estate

Agents who are members of the National Association of Realtors are eligible to use the term "Realtor" in their professional vocabularies (NAR). Realtors are required to abide by a code of ethics and standards of practise, and the National Association of Realtors (NAR) gives them access to a wide variety of resources and services to assist them in meeting these obligations.

Chapter 4
National Principles

When discussing real estate, the term "national principles" refers to a collection of rules, regulations, and standards that are used to manage the real estate market in a certain nation. In addition to safeguarding the rights of property owners, purchasers, and tenants, the goals of these principles are to make the real estate market more open, honest, and competitive. The guiding principles address a wide variety of topics, including property rights, contract law, zoning and land use rules, taxes, environmental regulations, consumer protection, and alternative dispute resolution. These guiding principles guarantee that transactions involving real estate are carried out in a manner that is compliant with the laws and regulations of the nation, and that the interests of all parties engaged in the transaction are safeguarded. They play a significant part in preserving the market's stability and trust, as well as ensuring that it functions in an effective and equitable manner, which are all critically important roles.

those principles aim to ensure the protection of property rights and provide a fair and transparent real estate market for all participants.

Property Rights

Individuals have the right to own, use, and transfer property, which is referred to as property rights in the context of real estate. These rights are the bedrock upon which real estate transactions are built, and they play an essential part in maintaining confidence and steadiness in the real estate market.

Right to Own Property

Real estate property rights include the right of individuals to own property, which provides them the capacity to govern and make choices regarding the property. This right to own property is also known as the "right of occupancy." This includes the ability to sell, lease, or otherwise transfer the property to third parties.

Property rights also include the right to use the property in whatever manner the owner deems appropriate, subject to certain limits. This ability to utilise the property is included in property rights. This may include the right to utilise the property for either residential or commercial reasons, as well as agricultural uses.

Right to Transfer Property rights also include the right to transfer property, which can occur through the sale of the property, the gifting of the property, or the inheritance of the property. Because of this, people can leave their property to their heirs or transfer it to other people in whichever manner they see appropriate.

Taxation on Real Estate

Property rights in real estate also include the right to pay property taxes, which are charged by the government to support public services and are collected to generate revenue for those services. Property taxes are one of the most important sources of revenue for many different governments and are normally calculated depending on the value of the property.

The area of the law that is concerned with issues pertaining to property ownership and usage is known as property law. This area of the law governs property rights in real estate and is a subfield of real estate law. The laws and processes for purchasing, selling, and transferring property are outlined in property law, and the law also offers a framework for the resolution of disputes that arise between parties.

Zoning and Land Use Laws

Property rights in real estate are also regulated by zoning and land use regulations, which govern how properties may be used and developed. Zoning and land use regulations are responsible for deciding how properties can be used and developed. These laws can have an effect not only on the value of the property but also on the ways in which it can be used, such as whether it can be used for residential or commercial reasons.

Eminent Domain

The government can seize private property for the purpose of putting it to public use, such as the construction of roads, schools, or public parks, and in some circumstances, it may exercise this power. In situations like these, the government is obligated to give the owner of the land with fair recompense.

When it comes to maintaining confidence and steadiness in the real estate market, property rights in real estate play an extremely important role. Individuals get the ability to control and make decisions regarding their property because of these rights, as well as the freedom to use it as they see appropriate and to transfer it to others. Property rights are controlled by property law and are subject to certain constraints, such as zoning and land use rules and the power of eminent domain. Property law also determines whether a person can transfer their property rights to another person. It is necessary for individuals who are involved in real estate transactions, as well as for maintaining the integrity of the real estate market, to have a solid understanding of property rights and to take appropriate measures to defend those rights.

Contract Law

Contract law in real estate refers to the body of legal principles that regulate the creation and enforcement of contracts between buyers, sellers, and tenants in real estate transactions. Contract law also includes the rights and responsibilities of the parties involved in these transactions. Contract law is an integral part of real estate transactions and plays an important part in preserving the market's stability and confidence level.

Contract Formation

Real estate contract law lays forth the principles for the formation of contracts, including the necessity that an offer and acceptance, consideration, and mutual agreement must be present before a contract may be considered formed. When it comes to dealings involving real estate, a contract is often established when a buyer agrees to purchase a property from a seller or when a tenant agrees to rent a property from a landlord. Both events constitute a binding agreement between the parties involved.

The parties to the agreement are required to reach a consensus on the terms of the contract, which must be unambiguous and detailed.

Performance and Enforcement

Real estate transaction law, which includes contract law, is what controls both the performance of contracts and their enforcement. This encompasses both the responsibility of the parties to perform their contractual commitments as well as the remedies that are available to the parties if a breach of contract has occurred.

Contract Law in Real Estate

The contract law that governs real estate relates to a broad variety of real estate transactions, such as the buying and selling of properties, the leasing of properties, and the transfer of property rights.

Statute of Frauds

Contract law in real estate also includes the Statute of Frauds, which requires certain types of contracts, such as contracts for the sale of real property, to be written down for them to be enforceable. Examples of these types of contracts include sales agreements for real estate.

Consumer Protection

Real estate contract law also includes measures for consumer protection, the purpose of which is to protect purchasers and tenants from unfair or misleading business practises.

The importance of real estate contract law cannot be overstated when it comes to maintaining confidence and steadiness in the real estate market. When it comes to real estate transactions, the formulation, terms, performance, and enforcement of contracts are all governed by the legal principles of contract law. These rules also provide a framework for mediating disagreements between parties. The persons who are involved in real estate transactions, as well as those who are responsible for preserving the integrity of the real estate market, need to have a solid understanding of contract law.

Zoning and Land Use Regulations:

When discussing real estate, the terms "zoning" and "land use rules" refer to the laws and policies that control the use of property and how it can be developed within a certain jurisdiction. These rules are an essential component of the real estate market because of the significant influence they play in determining the nature and purpose of real estate and because of the market's overall importance.

Zoning and land use rules serve the purpose of promoting public health, safety, and welfare by managing the use and development of property. This is done through a process known as "controlling the use and development of land." These regulations can specify the kinds of uses that are allowed in a particular area, such as residential, commercial, or industrial uses, and they can also regulate the intensity of use, such as the height, size, and placement of buildings. For example, residential uses can be allowed in an area, but commercial and industrial uses cannot.

Ordinances Relating to Zoning

Zoning ordinances are the legal documents that are used to put zoning and land use restrictions into effect. Ordinances such as these are often passed by local governments and serve to split a jurisdiction into several distinct zoning districts, each of which is responsible for the establishment and use of its own rules.

Plans for Land Use

Zoning and land use rules sometimes contain land use plans as well. Land use plans are all-encompassing documents that define the potential future growth of a jurisdiction. These plans may cover a wide variety of concerns, such as the patterns of land use, the transportation systems, the preservation of the environment, and the community amenities.

People or groups may seek to have a property rezoned to allow for a new use or development pattern. Zoning and land use restrictions are subject to change, and individuals or organisations may seek to have a property rezoned. The procedure of rezoning normally requires a public hearing and evaluation by the local government. Additionally, the decision to accept or refuse a rezoning request is susceptible to appeal.

Variances: Zoning and land use laws can also be amended by the issuing of variances, which are exceptions to the regulations that allow for a specific use or development pattern. Variances are an additional method by which zoning, and land use regulations can be modified. In most cases, a variance will be granted in response to a specific, one-of-a-kind condition, such as an unfair hardship or burden imposed on the property owner.

As a result, zoning and land use regulations can affect property values. A change in zoning, for instance, that enables higher-density development might lead to a rise in the value of a property. On the other hand, a change in zoning that restricts usage can lead to a fall in the value of a property.

Legal Challenges

Zoning and land use restrictions can be legally challenged, and individuals or groups can file lawsuits challenging the legitimacy or application of these regulations. These challenges may address a broad variety of problems, some of which include the legality of the rules, the fairness of the decision-making process, and the impact of the restrictions on property rights.

Regulations on zoning and land use play a significant part in the formation of the personality and purpose of real estate, as well as in the advancement of public health, safety, and welfare.

Taxation

Taxation in real estate refers to the many different types of taxes that can be levied on real property as well as transactions involving real property. In addition to being an essential component of the overall real estate industry, these taxes are also an essential factor in the funding of both regional and national governments.

Taxes on Real Estate

Property taxes are the most prevalent form of tax that is levied on real estate, and they are normally calculated based on the property's assessed value. Property taxes are often charged by municipal governments, and the revenue collected from them is utilised to finance a diverse array of public services, such as those provided by the police and the fire department.

Transfer taxes are taxes that are levied on the transfer of ownership of real property, and they are often calculated as a percentage of the selling price of the property. Taxes on transfers can be levied by municipal, state, or national governments, and they have the potential to be large for transactions involving a high value.

Taxes on Estates

Estate taxes are taxes that are levied on the transfer of real property upon the death of the owner, and they are often calculated as a percentage of the property's value. These taxes are known as "death taxes." When it comes to estate planning, estate taxes can be a significant consideration since they are susceptible to a wide variety of deductions and exclusions.

Taxes on Sales

Taxes that are levied on the sale of real estate are referred to as sales taxes, and they are often calculated as a percentage of the selling price. Most of the time, state governments are the ones that levy sales taxes, and these levies can be rather different from one jurisdiction to the next.

Tax Deductions

The ability to claim a tax deduction for expenses related to real estate ownership can result in substantial tax savings for both individuals and businesses. These deductions can include things like interest paid on a mortgage, taxes paid on the property, depreciation, and a range of other costs associated with owning and running a piece of real estate.

Tax credits

Tax credits for real estate can also give considerable tax savings for individuals as well as companies. These tax credits can be utilised to offset taxes that are owing or to earn a tax refund. Tax credits for real estate might include benefits for a variety of different things, including energy-efficient upgrades, low-income housing, historic preservation, and more.

Tax Controversies

The subject of real estate taxation is one that is intricate and frequently contentious, and disagreements about taxes can occur between taxpayers and government organisations. Tax disagreements can centre on a broad variety of topics, such as the assessment of a property's value, the determination of the amount of taxes that are owing, and the interpretation of relevant tax laws and regulations.

Taxation is an essential component in the process of financing both local and national governments, as well as in the process of forming the housing market. Individuals who are involved in real estate transactions, as well as those who want to make the most of the benefits that come with owning and running real estate, absolutely need to have a solid understanding of the numerous taxes that are levied on real state. Real state is a complicated system, and successfully navigating it involves understanding of the many tax rules and regulations, as well as the capacity to efficiently manage tax responsibilities and take advantage of chances to save money on taxes.

Environmental Regulations

Regulations pertaining to the environment play an essential part in the real estate sector since they serve to safeguard both public health and the natural environment, in addition to assuring the viability and accountability of any construction projects that are undertaken. Real estate developers and property owners in many different jurisdictions are subject to a broad variety of environmental restrictions, which can have a variety of different effects on the projects they are working on.

Zoning Rules

Local governments employ zoning regulations to restrict how land may be used, and these regulations frequently play a substantial influence in deciding what kinds of development projects are allowed in each area. Zoning regulations are used to regulate the use of land. Zoning laws can be used to preserve environmental resources like wetlands, forests, and animal habitats, in addition to controlling the kind of development projects, their scale, and where they are built. Zoning restrictions can also be used to manage the placement of development projects.

Environmental Impact Assessments (EIAs) are analyses of the possible environmental implications of a development project, and they are frequently mandated by local, state, or national governments. These evaluations may be found in environmental impact assessments (EIAs). EIAs can be utilised to assess the impacts of development projects on the quality of the air and water, as well as the wildlife and habitat, and other environmental resources. Additionally, EIAs can be utilised to inform decision-making and ensure that projects are developed in a manner that is both responsible and sustainable.

Air and Water Pollution Laws

The purpose of air and water pollution regulations is to preserve human health and the environment by controlling the discharge of pollutants into the air and water. These regulations are used to restrict the discharge of pollutants. These requirements must be complied with by real estate developers and property owners, who are also required to take measures to avoid or minimise the discharge of pollutants from their premises.

Hazardous Waste Rules

Hazardous waste regulations are meant to safeguard both public health and the environment, and they are used to manage the storage, transportation, and disposal of hazardous waste items. The developers of real estate and property owners are required to comply with these requirements, and they are also required to take measures to either avoid the presence of hazardous waste items on their premises or manage those that are already there.

Regulations for Protecting Endangered Species

The regulations for protecting endangered species are put in place to safeguard species that are threatened or endangered with extinction, and they can also play an important part. Additionally, they are obligated to take measures to safeguard endangered species and the habitats in which they live, as well as to guarantee that development projects do not do any harm to these species.

Regulations for Historic Preservation

Historic preservation regulations are put in place to safeguard cultural and historical treasures, and they also have the potential to have a substantial impact on the expansion of real estate projects. Developers of real estate and property owners are required to comply with these requirements. Additionally, they are obligated to take measures to conserve and safeguard historic resources, as well as to guarantee that development initiatives do not cause harm to these resources.

Regulations Regarding Climate Change

Regulations regarding climate change are used to combat the effects of climate change, and they may also play a vital role in the development of real estate. Real estate developers and property owners are required to comply with these regulations. Additionally, they are obligated to take measures to reduce emissions of greenhouse gases, to mitigate the effects of climate change, and to ensure that their properties are resilient to the effects of climate change.

Chapter 5

Financial Aspects

The term "financial elements" refers to a wide variety of key features that influence the financial success of real estate investments. These components are included in real estate transactions. These factors are as follows:

Investment Cost

Investment Investing in real estate requires careful consideration of the cost involved. This refers to the total cost of purchasing a property, which incorporates all the expenditures related with the transaction, such as those associated with the closing, any legal fees, and the cost of any necessary repairs or modifications. When evaluating the overall financial success of a real estate investment, it is vital to have a solid understanding of the costs associated with the transaction.

When considering whether to invest in real estate, there are many kinds of expenses that need to be accounted for. These are the following:

The purchase price

The purchase price is the total amount that must be paid to acquire the property, considering any discounts or premiums that were agreed.

Closing expenses

Closing expenses are fees that are involved with the process of transferring ownership of a property from one party to another. These expenditures could include escrow fees, legal fees, title insurance premiums, and other administrative expenses as well.

Renovations and Repairs

Before a property can be occupied, it may require renovations and repairs. The expenditures associated with these activities need to be figured into the total cost of the investment. This might encompass anything from simple upgrades to the aesthetics to extensive repairs to the structure.

Holding costs are expenses that are incurred when a property is being kept prior to it being sold or rented out. Holding costs are also known as storage charges. Among these are things like property taxes, insurance premiums, and repair and maintenance fees.

Financing charges

The fees that are incurred in the process of acquiring a mortgage or other kind of financing for a piece of real estate are referred to as financing charges. This may include fees for the origination of the loan, charges associated with the closing, and interest payments.

When determining the financial performance of a real estate investment, the cost of the investment is an essential component to take into consideration. When all the expenditures that relate to an investment are taken into consideration, a property that looks to be a good value on the surface may not be that good of a deal after all. When attempting to analyse the total financial success of a real estate investment, investors need consider not just the investment cost but also several other financial elements, such as cash flow, depreciation, and appreciation.

The return on investment (ROI), which calculates the total net profit of an investment as a percentage of the total cost of the investment, is an additional factor that should not be overlooked. A low ROI signifies that the investment may not be functioning as well as planned, whereas a high ROI indicates a higher degree of profitability than would be indicated by the low ROI. Investors should carefully examine the cost of investments and consider the possible influence that holding costs, financing costs, and other expenditures may have on the overall financial performance of the investment to optimise their return on investment (ROI).

When considering possible investments, it is important to give serious consideration to the cost of the investment, which is a crucial consideration in real estate investments. Investors should work with financial advisors to determine the potential impact that a wide range of costs associated with real estate investments may have on the overall financial performance of their investments and to gain an understanding of the full range of costs associated with real estate investments.

Financing

When it comes to investing in real estate, financing is an essential component since it has the potential to influence both the total return on investment (ROI) and the financial performance of a property. Real estate investors have access to a diverse range of funding choices, including conventional mortgage loans, alternative financing options such as hard money loans, and private equity investments. It is crucial for real estate investors to have a solid understanding of the many financing choices available.

Conventional mortgage loans are the most prevalent kind of financing utilised for real estate ventures. Mortgage loans are secured by the property that is being purchased and may often be obtained through financial organisations such as banks or other lending institutions. It is possible for the terms and circumstances of a mortgage loan to be very different from one another, but in most cases, the loan will include a predetermined interest rate, a predetermined amount of time for repayment, and a need that a down payment be made.

Loans Against Hard Money

Hard money loans are a form of alternative financing that are typically utilised for investments that are only held for a brief period or for properties that might not qualify for conventional mortgage loans. Private investors are the most common source of hard money loans, and the collateral for these loans is often the property that is being acquired. The terms and conditions of hard money loans are frequently more flexible than those of conventional mortgage loans; nonetheless, hard money loans generally have higher interest rates and shorter payback periods than conventional mortgage loans.

Private equity

Private equity is a term used to describe investment money that comes from private sources such as people or companies that specialise in private investments. Many other kinds of real estate investments, such as the purchase of existing properties, the construction of new buildings, and the refurbishment of existing ones, can all make use of private equity. It is possible for the terms and circumstances of private equity investments to range greatly, but in most cases, the investor will be expected to make an initial commitment that is substantial and will get a portion of the profits that are created by the venture.

Tax credits, grants, and loans with low interest rates are only some of the numerous financial instruments and programmes that may be utilised to fund real estate investments in addition to the possibilities for financing real estate transactions.

When considering the various financing options for an investment in real estate, it is essential to consider the effect that the terms and conditions of the financing will have on the overall financial performance of the investment. This is because the terms and conditions of the financing will dictate how much money the investor will have access to. This comprises the interest rate, the length of time during which the debt must be repaid, and any fees or other costs that are linked with the financing.

The total effect that financing has on the return on investment (ROI) is another essential factor to consider. The total return on investment (ROI) of an investment may be increased, for instance, if the interest rate is lower, whereas the ROI may be decreased if the interest rate is higher. In addition, the terms, and circumstances of the financing, such as the payback time and any fees or penalties, can also influence the return on investment (ROI).

Finance is an essential component of investing in real estate, and investors should carefully assess the many financing choices available to them to select the most appropriate financing plan for their respective assets. Investors should work with financial advisors to maximise the return on investment (ROI) of their real estate investments, to understand the terms and conditions of the various financing options, to determine the impact that financing will have on the overall financial performance of their investments, and to determine the impact that financing will have on the overall financial performance of their investments.

Cash Flow

The property's ability to generate positive cash flow is one of the most significant factors in determining whether an investment property will be profitable over the long run. Cash flow is a property's lifeblood. A property's cash flow is the amount of money that is created by the property, less any expenditures that are related with owning and maintaining the property. Cash flow is an important measure of a property's profitability. It is essential for real estate investors to have a solid understanding of cash flow since it has the potential to influence both the total return on investment (ROI) and the financial performance of a property.

Having a Solid Understanding of Cash Flow In order to have a solid understanding of cash flow, it is essential to evaluate the two primary components of cash flow, which are revenue and costs. The term "income" refers to not just the rent that is collected from renters but also any additional sources of income, such as fees for parking, laundry, and late payments. Expenses encompass all the expenditures connected with owning and maintaining the property, such as the monthly mortgage payment, property taxes, insurance, upkeep, and utility bills.

A property is said to have positive cash flow when the income generated by the property is greater than the costs associated with owning and operating the property. A property is said to have negative cash flow when the income generated by the property is less than the costs associated with owning and operating the property. When the costs of owning and managing a property are more than the revenue generated by the property, we say that the property has negative cash flow. This can happen when expenses are higher than income. Cash flow that is positive is typically seen as desirable since it enables the investor to generate a consistent stream of revenue and contributes to the property's ability to maintain its financial health over the long term.

The rental rate that is charged to tenants, the occupancy rate of the property, and the operating expenses that are associated with owning and operating the property are some of the factors that can impact a property's cash flow. Other factors that can impact cash flow include the number of days that a property is rented out. When determining the prospective cash flow of a property, it is essential to consider the aspects, since their effects on the property's overall financial performance might be considerable and should be considered.

Forecasting Cash Flow

In order to calculate the potential cash flow that may be generated by a piece of real estate, it is necessary to forecast both the revenue and costs that are connected to the property. Either by analysing previous financial data, such as rent rolls and operational expenditure records, or by utilising market data to anticipate the possible revenue and expenses connected with the property, this may be accomplished. Both methods are viable options. When calculating the prospective return on investment of an investment and the financial performance of a property, one of the most important steps to do is to make a cash flow projection.

Cash Flow Management

Once an investment property has been purchased, the cash flow of that property must be managed effectively to assure the property's continued sound financial health over the long term. This might involve lowering the property's operational expenditures, charging more rent to renters, or boosting the property's occupancy rate to a higher percentage of its available units. It is vital to perform consistent monitoring of a property's cash flow to guarantee that it will continue to maintain its sound financial health throughout time.

The property's ability to generate cash flow is an important feature to consider when investing in real estate since it is necessary for assuring the property's continued financial health over the long run. It is essential for real estate investors to have a solid understanding of the components that make up cash flow, the factors that influence cash flow, and the strategies for estimating and controlling cash flow. Real estate investors can optimise the return on investment (ROI) of their investments and assure the long-term financial success of their properties if they monitor and manage the cash flow of their buildings.

Appreciation

The term "appreciation" refers to a growth in the value of a property over the course of time and is one of the most important aspects of real estate investing. Appreciation is an essential consideration for real estate investors because it has the potential to boost a property's total return on investment (ROI) and contribute to the property's continued financial success over the long run.

Understanding Appreciation refers to an increase in the value of a property over a period. This increase in value can be caused by several different factors, including shifts in the real estate market, improvements made to the property, or increases in the demand for real estate in the area. An increase in a property's value might be the result of a variety of different circumstances, such as an improving local economy, shifting demographics, or shifting conditions in the real estate market.

Putting Appreciation into Perspective: Appreciation is often evaluated over a period, which might be as short as one year or if several years. It is required to compare the present market worth of a property to the price at which it was originally purchased or to the value of the property at a prior point in time to accurately estimate appreciation. The amount of appreciation that has taken place may be calculated as the difference in value between these two points in time.

Appreciation is influenced by the following factors: The value of a piece of real estate can be affected by a variety of variables, such as its location, the state of the economy, and the kinds of modifications that have been made to it. Location is one of the most important aspects to consider when buying real estate since homes located in desired regions are more likely to increase in value over time. The state of the economy can also have an effect, since a healthy economy can boost the demand for real estate, which in turn can lead to price rise. The value of a property may be increased by making investments in its repair and enhancement; therefore, property improvements can also influence the appreciation of the property.

The process of projecting a property's appreciation can be challenging since it is based on a wide variety of elements that are subject to shifts as the passage of time progresses. However, it is feasible to predict the probable appreciation of a property based on the present market circumstances, demographic trends, and the general situation of the economy. This may be done by using a combination of these factors. Investors may benefit from the expertise provided by real estate specialists and market analysts regarding the possibility for appreciation, which in turn enables them to make more educated decisions regarding their investments.

The Importance of Capital Appreciation

When Investing in Real Estate: Appreciation is an essential component for real estate investors because it has the potential to boost the overall return on investment (ROI) of a property and contribute to the profitability of the investment over the long run. Properties that have the potential for high levels of appreciation, such as those located in desired areas or those that may be enhanced via renovations or improvements, are good options for investors who are looking to maximise the returns on their investments.

The term "appreciation" refers to a growth in the value of a property over the course of time and is one of the most important aspects of real estate investing. Real estate investors should make it a priority to get an understanding of the elements that influence appreciation, as well as the methodologies for predicting appreciation and making the most of it. Real estate owners may optimise the return on their investments and assure the long-term financial success of their properties if they evaluate possible investments while also considering the possibility that the property's value would increase over time.

Market Conditions

Conditions in the market play an important part in the real estate sector, influencing a wide range of factors, including property values and the demand for real estate, as well as the sorts of properties that are being created and the state of the real estate market. It is necessary for real estate professionals, as well as for anybody intending to invest in the real estate market, to have a solid understanding of the major elements that have an influence on the current market circumstances.

Statistics of the Economic Climate Real estate market conditions are significantly influenced by a wide range of economic indicators, including unemployment rates, inflation rates, and gross domestic product (GDP). People who are confident in their work situation and have an adequate amount of discretionary income are more inclined to put their money into real estate investments. A robust economy can help fuel demand for real estate because of this. On the other side, a downturn in the economy may result in a decrease in demand for real estate as individuals become warier about their ability to make profitable investments.

Rates of Interest The prevailing rates of interest also play a crucial part in determining the circumstances of the real estate market. Mortgages are made cheaper for consumers to take out when interest rates are low, which can lead to an increase in the demand for real estate. On the other hand, consumers may be dissuaded from taking out mortgages when interest rates are high, which can result in a decrease in the market for real estate.

Demographic Trends:

Market conditions in the real estate business can be impacted by demographic trends such as population growth, ageing populations, and migration patterns. For instance, an increase in the population might result in an increase in the demand for housing and a rise in the level of competition for properties, but an ageing population may result in a decrease in the demand for housing as individuals move into retirement communities or downsize their homes.

Supply and Demand:

The equilibrium that exists between supply and demand is another significant aspect that influences the dynamics of the real estate market. Prices have the potential to rise when there is a high demand for real estate, while prices may fall when there is an excess supply of available homes. To make educated choices regarding the real estate market, real estate professionals need to have a constant awareness of the shifts that occur in supply and demand.

Circumstances in the local market the market conditions can differ significantly from one area to another, and even from one city to another. Real estate professionals should make it a priority to gain a comprehensive understanding of the market conditions that exist in any given location. This provides them with the information necessary to make educated choices regarding investments and to concentrate their efforts in those areas where they are most likely to be fruitful.

Conditions in the market play an important part in the real estate sector, influencing a wide range of factors, including property values and the demand for real estate, as well as the sorts of properties that are being created and the state of the real estate market. Real estate professionals and investors can make educated decisions regarding their investments and maximise their level of success in the real estate market if they maintain a heightened awareness of the key factors that influence market conditions. These key factors include economic indicators, interest rates, demographic trends, supply and demand, and local market conditions.

Chapter 6

Legal aspects and contract types

A sizeable percentage of the real estate sector is taken up by the many legal concerns that are associated with real estate transactions. Real estate agents need to have a full grasp of the rules and regulations that govern the purchasing, selling, and renting of properties so that they may provide the best possible service to their consumers.

Two of the most important aspects of real estate transactions from a legal standpoint are the initial creation of contracts and the later fulfilment of the obligations outlined in those contracts. Contracts such as purchase agreements, listing agreements, and lease agreements are commonplace in the real estate industry, and it is required of real estate agents that they be familiar with all these different kinds of contracts. In addition, it is essential for them to understand the terms and conditions that need to be incorporated into these contracts in order for them to be legally binding and enforceable.

The closure of the transaction and the administration of the escrow account are two additional legally crucial parts of purchasing real estate. It is essential for real estate professionals to have a solid understanding of the escrow process and the roles that each participant, including the buyer, the seller, and the escrow agent, plays in the transaction. This includes having a clear understanding of the responsibilities that the escrow agent has. In addition to this, they should be familiar with the process of closure, which involves a variety of procedures such as the creation of closing papers, the transfer of title, and the distribution of cash, among other activities.

Real estate agents are required to have an in-depth understanding of a wide variety of additional legal concerns that may come up during the buying, selling, and renting of properties. In addition to these aspects of real estate transactions, real estate agents are required to have an in-depth understanding of these additional legal concerns. Some examples of these challenges are as follows: This includes issues relating to zoning, land use, and environmental regulations, as well as fair housing laws, which prohibit discrimination in housing based on race, colour, national origin, religion, sex, familial status, and disability. Other relevant laws include the Americans with Disabilities Act and the National Environmental Policy Act. Laws that ban discrimination in housing based on family status are another example of the type of legislation that falls under this category.

Knowledge of the laws and regulations that control the advertising and marketing of properties, including the restrictions that pertain to open houses, signage, and other promotional materials, is another requirement for the profession of real estate agent. This knowledge is necessary because open houses, signage, and other promotional materials are governed by these laws and regulations. In addition, it is necessary for them to understand the rules and regulations that are associated with privacy, the protection of data, and cybersecurity, all of which are becoming increasingly important in this age of digital technology.

It is necessary to have an in-depth expertise with the numerous rules and regulations that govern the real estate industry to successfully manage the legal aspects of real estate transactions, which are notoriously tough to navigate. When it comes to buying, selling, or renting a property, a wide variety of legal concerns may arise. Real estate agents are required to have a working knowledge of all the many types of contracts that are common in the field, as well as the procedures for managing escrow and closing. In addition, they are required to have a complete understanding of the real estate industry. By staying current on the numerous legal problems that are relevant to the real estate sector, real estate agents may better serve their clients' interests and help them achieve a successful and trouble-free finish to their real estate transactions.

The real estate industry makes use of a variety of contracts and agreements, the most common of which being leases, listing agreements, and purchase agreements.

Purchase Agreement:

A A Purchase Agreement is a legal document that specifies the terms and conditions of a real estate transaction between a buyer and a seller. This agreement is made between the buyer and the seller of the property. Both parties are required to physically sign this legally binding agreement for it to take effect. In most situations, it will include crucial particulars such as the purchase price, the financing conditions, the closing date, and any contingencies that need to be met before the transaction can be finalised.

One of the most significant components of an Acquisition Agreement is the price that has been agreed upon for the purchase. The agreement reached between the buyer and the seller regarding the total amount that the buyer would pay for the property is referred to as the purchase price, and it is customarily reached because of discussions between the buyer and the seller. It is possible for the purchase price to be a set amount of money that has been decided upon ahead of time, or it may be contingent on the fulfilment of criteria, such as the outcomes of a home inspection or appraisal.

A Purchase Agreement should always include a section describing the terms and conditions of the financing arrangement. This addresses the type of loan that the purchaser will use to finance the purchase, the interest rate that will be applied to the loan, and the length of time that the loan will be in effect for the purchaser. If the buyer intends to get financing for the purchase of the property, then the Purchase Agreement must contain a language that gives the mortgage lender the right to review the terms of the agreement.

A Purchase Agreement must also provide the date that the transaction will be closed, as this is an essential part of the agreement. This is the day that the buyer will get title to the property, and it is also the day on which the sale of the property will be regarded as having been effectively concluded. The buyer and the seller are required to come to an understanding on the timing of the closure, which typically takes place several weeks after the signing of the Purchase Agreement.

Contingencies are conditions and requirements that need to be fulfilled before the transaction can be finalised. In addition to these basic components, a Purchase Agreement may also include contingencies, which are terms and prerequisites that need to be satisfied. For instance, one kind of contingency that is rather common is a house inspection contingency clause. Because of this clause, the buyer can have the property evaluated by an experienced inspector in order to identify any potential problems. If the home inspector finds any issues with the property that are deemed to be unacceptable, the buyer has the right to either renegotiate the purchase price or back out of the arrangement.

Listing Agreement:

A Listing Agreement, also known as a Listing Contract, is a document that is legally enforceable between a real estate agent and a property owner that describes the terms and circumstances of the sale or lease of a property. This contract may also be referred to as a Listing Contract. The agreement specifies the duties of both parties, as well as the duration of the contract, the commission that is owed to the agent, and other elements pertaining to the purchase or lease of the property.

In most cases, a Listing Agreement will require the property owner to provide the broker the exclusive right to sell or lease the property for a certain amount of time. This can be done either temporarily or permanently. During this period, the broker will be actively seeking a buyer or tenant for the property as well as marketing the home in question. If the property is successfully leased or sold, the broker will be compensated with a commission as payment for the services they provided.

The following is a list of some of the most important components that must be incorporated into a

Listing Agreement:

The address of the property, a description of the property, and any other pertinent information about the property, such as the square footage, number of bedrooms and bathrooms, etc., should all be included in this part.

This section describes the duration of time that the Listing Agreement will be in force and is referred to as the Listing Period. It is standard practise for Listing Agreements to be valid for a certain amount of time, such as three or six months, after which they can be extended if the property in question has not been bought or rented by the time the term comes to an end.

Commission:

This section specifies the commission that will be given to the broker if the property is leased or sold after it has been listed. The owner of the property is responsible for paying the commission, which is often expressed as a percentage of the total price of the sale or lease.

Marketing and Advertising:

The measures that the agent will take to market the property are outlined in this section. These procedures include advertising, open houses, and other means of reaching potential purchasers or tenants.

In the section under "Representation," the duties and obligations of the broker in terms of representing the property owner and the property itself are laid forth. In addition to guiding and advising the owner of the property, the agent is accountable for negotiating the purchase or lease of the property.

Termination

This section specifies the terms under which the Listing Agreement can be terminated by any party at their discretion at any time during the period of the agreement. Usually, one party may cancel the agreement at any time by providing writing notice to the other party.

Dispute Resolution:

This section covers the process for addressing any problems that may develop between the property owner and the agent. Disputes may arise for several reasons, including but not limited to: Most disagreements are settled by some form of mediation or arbitration.

Legal Compliance:

This section covers the responsibility of both parties to comply with all applicable laws and regulations, including fair housing legislation and anti-discrimination statutes, as well as any other laws that may apply.

A listing agreement is an important contract that should not be overlooked by either property owners or real estate agents. It describes the duties of both parties, as well as the terms and conditions of the sale or lease of the property, and it defines those terms and circumstances. Before signing the Listing Agreement, it is essential to verify that the terms have been well reviewed and comprehended by oneself to guarantee that the agreement will serve both parties' needs in the most favourable manner possible.

Lease Agreement

The terms and circumstances of renting a property are spelled out in a document called a lease agreement, which is a contract between a landlord and a tenant that describes the terms and conditions of renting a property. A lease agreement is an essential document in the field of real estate since it guarantees that both parties are aware of their respective rights and responsibilities.

Information Regarding the Property

The name of the tenant, the name of the landlord, and the address of the property should all be included in the lease agreement. This part of the agreement lays the groundwork for the other parts of the agreement.

The length of the lease should be included in the lease agreement, together with the beginning and ending dates of the tenancy and an indication of whether it is a short-term or long-term lease. The notice time that is necessary for early termination should also be stated in the lease agreement.

The amount of rent, as well as the day on which it is due and the manner of payment, should all be included in the lease agreement. This section ought to additionally provide an explanation of any late fees or penalties that are imposed for non-payment.

Deposit of Security:

The amount of the security deposit and any conditions for its return, such as the state of the property at the conclusion of the lease, should be included in the lease agreement.

Utilities:

In the lease agreement, it should be specified which utilities (such as water, electricity, gas, and internet) are included in the rent, and which utilities are the responsibility of the tenant to pay for.

Repairs & Maintenance

The maintenance and repair obligations of the property should be outlined in the lease agreement, with both the landlord and the renter being held accountable. In this part, you should also identify who is responsible for making repairs to the property's various components, including appliances, fixtures, and other aspects.

Use of the Property

The lease agreement ought to detail the kinds of uses that are permitted for the property (e.g., residential, commercial, etc.). The agreement must include any limits on the usage of the property, like a no-smoking policy and a no-pets rule, for example.

When it comes to subleasing, the lease agreement should make it clear whether the tenant is permitted to do so and if so, under what terms and conditions.

Access

The lease agreement should detail the landlord's right to enter the property as well as the appropriate amount of advanced notice before the landlord can enter the property.

Termination: The lease agreement should detail the circumstances under which the tenancy can be ended, such as the tenant's failure to pay rent or a violation of the terms of the lease.

Resolution of Disputes

The rental agreement should detail how disagreements between the landlord and the tenant will be settled if they arise, offering options such as mediation or arbitration.

Renewal: The lease agreement should make clear whether or whether the tenant has the option to renew the lease, as well as the terms and conditions that apply to such a renewal.

Governing Law

The leasing agreement should make it clear whose laws will apply to the agreement and indicate which jurisdiction's laws will apply.

Signatures: Both the landlord and the tenant are required to sign the lease agreement to demonstrate that they have read, understood, and agree with the terms and conditions that are contained in the contract.

An important document that defines the terms and conditions of renting a property is called a lease agreement. Before signing a lease agreement, it is essential for both the landlord and the tenant to ensure that they have a complete understanding of its terms to prevent disagreements in the future. A lease agreement that is well-written may safeguard the interests of both parties and guarantee that the tenancy goes off without a hitch.

Rental Agreement:

A rental agreement, which may also be referred to as a lease agreement, is a legally binding contract that describes the terms and conditions of renting a property and is made between a landlord and a tenant. The document may also go by the name of a lease agreement. When it comes to real estate, a rental agreement is an essential piece of paperwork that lays the groundwork for a prosperous tenancy.

Details About the Rental Property The name of the tenant, the name of the landlord, and the address of the rental property should all be included in the rental agreement. This part of the agreement lays the groundwork for the other parts of the agreement.

The length of the lease should be included in the rental agreement, together with the beginning and ending dates of the tenancy and an indication of whether it is a short-term or long-term lease. In addition to this, the agreement must detail the mandatory notice time in the event of termination.

The amount of rent, as well as the day on which it is due and the manner of payment, should all be included in the rental agreement. This section ought to additionally provide an explanation of any late fees or penalties that are imposed for non-payment.

Deposit of Security

The amount of the security deposit, as well as any conditions for its return, such as the state of the property at the conclusion of the lease, should be included in the rental agreement.

Utilities

The rental agreement should indicate which utilities (such as water, electricity, gas, and internet) are included in the rent and which utilities the renter is responsible for paying for. The tenant's responsibility may include paying for water, electricity, gas, and internet.

Repairs and Maintenance

The maintenance and repair obligations of the property should be spelled out in the rental agreement for both the landlord and the tenant. In this part, you should also identify who is responsible for making repairs to the property's various components, including appliances, fixtures, and other aspects.

Use of the Property

The rental agreement ought to detail the kinds of uses that are permitted for the property (e.g., residential, commercial, etc.). The agreement must include any limits on the usage of the property, like a no-smoking policy and a no-pets rule, for example.

When it comes to subleasing, the rental agreement should make it clear whether the tenant is permitted to do so and if so, under what terms and conditions.

Access

The rental agreement should detail the landlord's right to access the property as well as the appropriate amount of advanced notice before the landlord can enter the rental unit.

The rental agreement should include a clause that specifies the grounds under which the tenancy can be terminated, such as the tenant's failure to pay rent or a violation of the terms of the agreement.

Resolution of Disputes

The rental agreement ought to include stipulations on the way disagreements between the landlord and the tenant will be settled, such as through mediation or arbitration.

Renewal

The rental agreement should make it clear whether the tenant has the option to renew the tenancy, as well as under what terms that choice is available to them.

The rental agreement must include a clause that identifies the laws of the jurisdiction that will govern the arrangement.

Signatures

Both the landlord and the tenant are required to sign the rental agreement to demonstrate their understanding and acceptance of the terms and conditions that are described in the contract.

The terms and conditions of renting a home are outlined in an important document called a rental agreement. Before signing the rental agreement, it is essential for both the landlord and the tenant to ensure that they have a complete understanding of its terms to prevent disagreements in the future. A rental agreement that is well-written may safeguard the interests of both parties and guarantee that the tenancy goes off without a hitch.

Option Agreement:

In the real estate industry, a contract between a property owner and a potential buyer is known as an option agreement. This type of agreement gives the buyer the right, but not the obligation, to purchase the property at a certain price and within a certain amount of time during the term of the agreement. The buyer has the option to acquire the property, and the option agreement spells out the terms and conditions that must be met before the buyer may exercise this option.

Information Relating to the Property

The option agreement must contain the address of the property, the name of the owner, as well as the name of the buyer. This part of the agreement lays the groundwork for the other parts of the agreement.

Option Price

The amount that the buyer is required to pay to get the right to purchase the property should be outlined in the option agreement. This payment, which acts as compensation for the seller granted the option, is normally non-refundable and is made in advance.

Option Period: The length of time that the buyer has the right to acquire the property should be specified in the option agreement as the length of time that the buyer has the option to purchase the property. This time frame is referred to as the option period.

Purchase Amount:

The price that the buyer will be required to pay to purchase the property if they exercise their option to do so should be specified in the option agreement. To compensate the seller for the opportunity cost of not being able to sell the property during the option period, this purchase price ought to be larger than the option price.

Requirements

The option agreement should contain any criteria that must be satisfied before the option may be exercised. Some examples of conditions include the buyer receiving financing or the buyer gaining clearance from a government agency.

Termination

The option agreement should include the conditions under which the option might be terminated, such as the buyer failing to pay the option price or the seller getting a superior offer from another bidder. These are both examples of situations in which the option could be cancelled.

The option agreement should clearly state the laws of the jurisdiction that will govern the agreement before it can be considered valid.

Signatures

The option agreement should be signed by both the owner and the buyer to express their agreement to the terms and conditions specified in the contract. The owner's signature should be placed on the bottom of the page.

A potential buyer in real estate is given the right, but not the responsibility, to acquire a property at a set price and within a specified amount of time provided the parties involved in the transaction enter into an option agreement. Both the buyer and the seller are safeguarded by the option agreement, which lays out the terms and conditions under which the option can be exercised and protects both parties. Before signing the option agreement, it is essential for both parties to ensure that they have a complete grasp of its terms. This will help to prevent disagreements in the future.

Chapter 7

Introduction about laws of most popular State

The regulations governing real estate licencing in each state are different, but you will likely need to be familiar with a few core concepts to pass a real estate agent test in any of the states that you specified. The following is a quick rundown of the criteria that are imposed by each state:

Georgia

You must be at least 21 years old, possess a high school diploma or an equivalent, finish a pre-licensing course that is at least 75 hours long, pass both a state and national exam, and apply to the Georgia Real Estate Commission to become a licenced real estate agent in Georgia.

New Jersey

To become a licenced real estate agent in the state of New Jersey, you need to be at least 18 years old, complete 75 hours of approved pre-licensing education, pass a state exam as well as a national exam, apply for a licence to the New Jersey Real Estate Commission, and complete an additional 45 hours of continuing education every two years.

Connecticut

You must be at least 18 years old, complete 40 hours of pre-licensing education, pass a state exam as well as a national exam, apply for a licence to the Connecticut Real Estate Commission, and complete continuing education every two years to keep your real estate licence in Connecticut.

New York

To become a licenced real estate agent in the state of New York, you need to be at least 18 years old, finish 75 hours of pre-licensing education, pass a state exam as well as a national exam, apply for a licence to the New York Department of State, and complete continuing education every two years to keep your licence active.

California

You must be at least 18 years old, complete 135 hours of pre-licensing education, pass a state exam as well as a national exam, apply for a licence to the California Bureau of Real Estate, and complete continuing education every four years to keep your licence active in the state of California.

Florida

In the state of Florida, to become a licenced real estate agent, you need to be at least 18 years old, complete 63 hours of pre-licensing education, pass a state exam as well as a national exam, apply for a licence to the Florida Department of Business and Professional Regulation, and complete continuing education every two years to keep your licence active.

Virginia

You must be at least 18 years old, complete 60 hours of pre-licensing education, pass a state exam as well as a national exam, submit a licence application to the Virginia Real Estate Board, and complete continuing education every two years to keep your real estate licence current in the state of Virginia.

Washington

To become a licenced real estate agent in the state of Washington, you need to be at least 18 years old, complete 90 hours of pre-licensing education, pass a state exam as well as a national exam, apply for a licence to the Washington State Department of Licensing, and continue your education every two years to keep your licence active.

Texas

To become a licenced real estate agent in the state of Texas, you need to be at least 18 years old, complete 180 hours of pre-licensing education, pass a state exam as well as a national exam, apply for a licence to the Texas Real Estate Commission, and complete continuing education at least once every two years to keep your licence active.

Illinois

You must be at least 21 years old, complete 75 hours of pre-licensing education, pass a state exam as well as a national exam, submit a licence application to the Illinois Department of Financial and Professional Regulation, and complete continuing education every two years to keep your real estate licence current in the state of Illinois.

South Carolina

To become a licenced real estate agent in South Carolina, you need to be at least 18 years old, complete 30 hours of pre-licensing education, pass a state exam as well as a national exam, apply for a licence to the South Carolina Real Estate Commission, and complete continuing education every two years in order to keep your licence active. are required to disclose any known flaws in the property.

North Carolina

You need to be at least 18 years old, complete 75 hours of pre-licensing education, pass a state exam as well as a national exam, submit a licence application to the North Carolina Real Estate Commission, and complete continuing education every two years to keep your real estate licence current in North Carolina.

Michigan

You must be at least 18 years old, complete 40 hours of pre-licensing education, pass a state exam as well as a national exam, submit a licence application to the Michigan Department of Licensing and Regulatory Affairs, and complete continuing education every two years to keep your real estate licence in Michigan.

Tennessee

You must be at least 18 years old, complete 60 hours of pre-licensing education, pass a state exam as well as a national exam, apply for a licence to the Tennessee Real Estate Commission, and complete continuing education every two years in order to keep your real estate licence in Tennessee.

Indiana

You must be at least 18 years old, complete 90 hours of pre-licensing education, pass a state exam as well as a national exam, submit a licence application to the Indiana Real Estate Commission, and complete continuing education every two years to keep your real estate licence current in Indiana.

Massachusetts

You must be at least 18 years old, complete 40 hours of pre-licensing education, pass a state exam as well as a national exam, submit a licence application to the Massachusetts Division of Professional Licensure, and complete continuing education every two years to keep your real estate agent licence in Massachusetts.

Chapter 8

Practice test

Study Materials Tailored to Each State The majority of states provide study materials that are tailored specifically to their real estate agent licencing examinations. These resources have the potential to serve as an excellent resource that will assist you in concentrating your studying efforts and gaining an understanding of the information that will be included on the examination.

Practice Examinations: There are a variety of real estate schools and websites that provide practise exams for the real estate agent licencing exam. Putting yourself through some practise exams is a great way to evaluate your current level of knowledge and pinpoint the subject matter on which you should concentrate your studies.

Participating in a study group with other people who are interested in a career in real estate may be an excellent method to keep oneself motivated and gain knowledge from the experiences of others.

1. You act as the seller's agent and sell the home for $135,000 in total. The commission rate that your brokerage charges is six percent, which is already factored into the selling price. The commission will be split 50/50 between the buyer's agent and the seller's agency. What percentage of the overall commission do you receive?

   a. $2,025

   b. $4,050

   c. $8,100

2. According to the zoning regulations in effect in your municipality, an apartment building must supply 2.5 parking spots for every 1,000 square feet of habitable area in the structure. The total floor space of an apartment complex in the neighbourhood is 20,000 square feet. How many parking spots do you think it ought to have?

   a. 40

   b. 50

   c. 45

   d. 55

3. Only when an FHA loan is being used to acquire the property does it become mandatory to declare whether the residence contains lead paint.

True

False

4. Which of the following out of the many costs associated with becoming a homeowner is eligible to be deducted from your taxable income?

    a. Property taxes

    b. Insurance

    c. Interest

    d. Both a and c

5. Assuming a rate of return of 12.5 percent, the monthly net income generated by an investment of $115,000 is _____.

    a. $1,150.00

    b. $7,666.67

    c. $1,197.92

    d. $14,375.00

6. You help a customer sell a house for which the down payment was $30,000, the loan amount was $125,000, the interest rate was 3.7%, and the duration of the loan was 30 years fixed. The monthly payment for the mortgage is now set at $1,219. What is the ratio of the loan to the property's value?

    a. .24

    b. .8

c. 1.62

d. 4.16

7. Your employer is the only party from which you are permitted to lawfully collect a commission.

True

False

8. The day began with a round of golf between the two managing brokers from separate brokerages. While playing a round of golf together in private, the two brokers concluded that the commission rates for the two brokerage businesses should be comparable to one another. The following is an illustration of:

a. Legal behaviour permitted in a free market economy.

b. Illegal behaviour under the Sherman Antitrust Act.

c. Illegal discrimination under federal fair housing laws.

d. Prohibited by the Statute of Frauds

9. Which aspects of real estate deals are covered under the Real Estate Settlement Procedures Act (RESPA)?

a. All cash sales

b. Sales involving seller financing

c. Federally related mortgage loans

d. All the above

10. It is necessary for a deed to be:

    a. Signed by the grantor

    b. Signed by the grantee

    c. Recorded at the state level.

    d. All the above.

11. When a real estate agent, broker, or lender engages in "blockbusting," they are trying to intimidate property owners in a community into selling their homes.

    True

    False

12. A buyer has submitted their application for an ARM loan. Do the monthly payments for this kind of loan package fluctuate at all?

    a. No. They stay the same over the course of the loan.

    b. Yes. The interest rate changes annually, either raising or lowering the payment.

    c. Yes. The interest rate goes up every year.

    d. Yes. The interest rate goes down every year.

13. How much time does a potential borrower have to evaluate the Closing Disclosure before it is considered acceptable?

    a. 1 business day before closing

    b. 2 business days before closing

c. 3 business days before closing

d. One week before closing

14. Some potential borrowers are denied loans from large financial institutions purely since the areas in which their properties are located are economically struggling. The lender accomplishes this goal by not taking into consideration either the state of the particular property being financed or the creditworthiness of the individual who is seeking to get financing. What exactly do you call this kind of criminal behaviour?

    a. Redlining

    b. Silent records

    c. Air loans

    d. Backward applications

15. You are attempting to determine the value of a property. It was sold for $125,000 exactly five years ago; nevertheless, property values in this specific neighbourhood have dropped by an average of 5% since then. What would you estimate the property to be worth roughly?

    a. $117,500

    b. $118,750

    c. $118,000

    d. $119,000

16. A homeowner often has a mortgage with an interest rate that is set in stone. What are the several ways that her payments might be adjusted?

a. None; the payment will not change over the life of the loan.

b. The property taxes go up or down.

c. The cost of homeowner's insurance goes up or down.

d. Either b or c.

17. A seller and a broker enter into a written listing agreement for the seller's 2-unit dwelling. The broker is authorized to advertise, stage, and solicit offers on the property. The broker's duties also include advising the seller as to the advantages and disadvantages of offers received. However, the broker cannot accept an offer and bind the seller. This is an example of what type of agency?

a. Special agency

b. General agency

c. Implied agency

d. Dual agency

18. Which of the following is protected by the federal Fair Housing Act?

a. Behaviour

b. Age

c. Marital Status

d. Minor children

19. A mortgagee's policy of title insurance is valid until:

a. The owner dies.

b. The owner sells the property.

c. The mortgagee neglects to renew the title insurance policy.

d. The loan is paid in full.

20. Which of the following components is NOT required for a contract to be considered valid?

    a. Consideration

    b. An offer and communicated acceptance

    c. A legal object of the contract

    d. All the above.

21. Who is permitted to properly assess a residential property if the transaction is going to be funded with a loan that is guaranteed by the FHA?

    a. The lender financing the purchase money mortgage

    b. A licensed appraiser

    c. A broker hired to provide a Broker Opinion of Value

    d. A home inspector.

22. All the following are excluded from the coverage provided by a standard owner's title insurance policy, except for.

    a. Forgery or fraud

    b. Improper delivery

    c. Lack of capacity

d. Building permit or zoning violations

23. What steps does a homeowner who is in the process of foreclosure need to do to exercise his right of redemption?

   a. Pay the entire mortgage

   b. Pay the entire mortgage, plus interest

   c. Pay the entire mortgage, plus court costs and legal fees

   d. Pay the entire mortgage, plus court costs, legal fees, and interest

24. Which of the following kind of mortgages will most likely have the market's most competitive beginning interest rate?

   a. Conventional 30-year fixed rate

   b. 30-year fixed rate FHA loan

   c. Conventional 15-year fixed rate

   d. Conventional 30-year ARM

25. A mother who owns a piece of real estate in severalty expresses the desire for her son to take possession of the land when she has passed away. Which of the following options is appropriate and will bring her the results she is looking for?

   a. A devise in a properly executed will.

   b. A life estate in which the son is the life tenant and measuring life, and the woman is the remainderman.

   c. Alienation via a delivered and accepted quitclaim deed.

d. Since the property is owned in severalty, the other owners will need to be consulted.

Answers:

1. b

2. b

3. False

4. d

5. c

6. b

7. True

8. b

9. c

10. a

11. True

12. b

13. c

14. a

15. b

16. d

17. a

18. d

19. d

20. d

21. b

22. d

23. d

24. d

25. a

Conclusion:

In conclusion, to obtain a licence to work as a real estate agent, one must first pass a test that is specific to the state in which they wish to work. The exam that one must pass to become a real estate agent includes a wide range of topics, including real estate legislation, financial ideas, and industry-specific vocabulary. Getting to prepare for the test, which should be your main goal, may be accomplished in an efficient manner in a number of different methods, including participating in study groups, studying materials that are specific to the state, and taking practise exams.

Even after they have received their licence, real estate agents are obliged to continue their education to remain in good standing. This includes satisfying any requirements for continuing education and ensuring that they are up to date on any changes that have occurred within the real estate industry or within the rules of the state in which they are licenced. Real estate agents are necessary to the functioning of the housing business because of the assistance they provide to clients throughout the home buying, selling, and renting processes. They are expected to comply with all applicable fair housing regulations, follow the highest ethical standards, and always operate in the best interests of the consumers.

Although being a real estate agent is not an easy road to take, it is one that, if pursued to completion, has the potential to be an exceptionally fulfilling and fruitful career decision. You will be better able to make a decision that is well-informed if you are familiar with the real estate agent test as well as the responsibilities that are associated with the position. This is true regardless of whether you are just starting out in your career or are considering making a career switch. Please leave a feedback of my book on Amazon to express your gratitude for it and how it has benefited you in all facets of your life.

Bonus

Top 3 software to automate all the real estate agent business

The following are the three best software choices for automating the business of real estate agents:

1. Contactually

This piece of software, known as Contactually, is intended to assist real estate professionals in managing their connections with leads and customers. It provides a centralised system for collecting and organising contact information, as well as capabilities for automated follow-up and communication with the contacts that are stored.

2. BrokerOffice

BrokerOffice is a piece of software that was developed with the sole purpose of meeting the needs of real estate brokerages. It offers a set of tools for managing agents, transactions, and contacts with customers. It is equipped with functions such as lead management and transaction management, in addition to a centralised database for the storage and organisation of information.

3. PlanPlus Online

This programme, known as PlanPlus Online, provides a full solution for real estate agents, including capabilities for lead generation, marketing, and customer relationship management. Among its other features, the software also manages client relationships. Additionally, it offers a mobile app that allows users to stay connected and productive even while they are on the move.

These software alternatives can help streamline many of the activities and procedures that are involved in running a real estate firm, allowing real estate agents to focus on doing what they are most skilled at, which is dealing with customers and making sales.

3 contents that will be indispensable for real estate agent career after passing the exam

After obtaining a passing score on the real estate test, there are a few important factors that must be maintained to have a successful career as a real estate agent. I'll give you three examples:

1. A Professional Website:

Currently, having a website that is both professional looking and easy to use is very necessary. Your website must prominently feature your listings, give information about your services, and make it simple for potential customers to get in touch with you.

2. Marketing Materials:

Marketing Materials Having a marketing materials portfolio that is professionally developed and well-planned, including business cards, flyers, and brochures, may help you make a strong first impression with clients and boost the exposure of your brand.

3. Networking Skills:

Abilities in Networking Because real estate is a people-driven profession, having excellent networking abilities might be the key to achieving success in the industry. You may increase the size of your client base, close more transactions, and produce more leads by cultivating relationships with other real estate agents, lenders, and home inspectors, as well as other industry experts.

You will have the foundation you need to build a successful and long-lasting career in real estate if you have these three things in place. These are the three things that are required.

References:

[r]. (n.d.). In *r*. Retrieved February 11, 2023, from https://www.tests.com/practice/real-estate-agent-test

Free Real Estate Agent Practice Test. (n.d.). In *Tests.com*. https://www.tests.com/practice/real-estate-agent-test

The typewriter trade in Scotland, from the 1870s to 1920s. https://nms.iro.bl.uk/concern/thesis_or_dissertations/63fc5f01-299f-4b24-9352-3f6dede311d3?locale=en

Boat Values - Boat Prices - Boat Valuation - BoatCrazy. https://boatcrazy.com/boat-values

So, what is the difference between a real estate agent and a property .... https://propertyalchemy.com.au/so-what-is-the-difference-between-a-real-estate-agent-and-a-property-manager/

The legal document that specifies the terms and conditions of a.... https://www.coursehero.com/tutors-problems/Financial-Accounting/39970843-The-legal-document-that-specifies-the-terms-and-conditions-of-a/

most significant factors in the - Traduzione in italiano - esempi .... https://context.reverso.net/traduzione/inglese-italiano/most+significant+factors+in+the

Transferring Ownership of Property: What You Need To Know. https://alattorneys.co.za/transferring-ownership-of-property-what-you-need-to-know-2/

"United Kingdom : Some Self-Employed Are Required to Comply with Anti-Money Laundering Laws." MENA Report, Albawaba (London) Ltd., 16 Nov. 2022.

What Are the Different Types of Taxes? | SoFi. https://www.sofi.com/learn/content/types-of-taxes/

Real Estate Finance 101: Four Types of Loan Closings. https://thomasandwebber.com/real-estate-finance-101-four-types-of-loan-closings/

Where Can You Buy Weed Online in Montreal? - ONLYGAS. https://onlygas.co/weed-blog/where-can-you-buy-weed-online-in-montreal/

How to Be a Successful Real Estate Agent: 10 Helpful Tips. https://realestateexamninja.com/how-to-be-a-successful-real-estate-agent/

List of plants in the family Rosaceae | Britannica. https://www.britannica.com/topic/list-of-plants-in-the-family-Rosaceae-2001612

The Best of the Best — Insights into Our 1st-Year Cover REALTORS®. https://www.realproducersmag.com/locations/carolina-coast-real-producers-d982/articles/-d3c425/

Real estate practise exam questions 1-50
https://www.youtube.com/watch?v=bEp-oYy9-RU

25 Questions You Will See on the Real Estate Exam
https://www.youtube.com/watch?v=_aAGenJjtDg

Made in the USA
Las Vegas, NV
02 June 2024

90621225R10057